SHARING THE ROAD WITH IDIOTS

BY

BOB GLICKMAN

Computer Illustrations (traffic signs & signals)
by WALTER N. STRUMP

Cover & Interior Cartoons
by DON SMITH

CCC Publications • Los Angeles

Published by

CCC Publications
9725 Lurline Avenue
Chatsworth, CA 91311

Manufactured in the United States of America
Cover © 1993 CCC Publications
Interior illustrations © 1993 CCC Publications
Cover & Interior cartoons by Don Smith
Computer illustrations (traffic signs & signals) by Walter N. Stump
Interior layout & production by Oasis Graphics

ISBN: 0-918259-55-X

If your local U.S. bookstore is out of stock, copies of this book may be obtained by mailing check or money order for $6.99 per book (plus $2.50 to cover postage and handling) to: CCC Publications; 9725 Lurline Avenue, Chatsworth, CA 91311

Pre-publication Edition - 8/93
First Printing - 3/94
Second Printing - 4/95
Third Printing - 10/96
Fourth Printing - 12/99

DEDICATION

*To the **best** "Best Friends" a person could ask for—*

Steve Streit, Al Cadwell, Luis Diaz, Randy James, Jim Grubbs, Scott Roberts, Andrea Hirsh, Jeff Korn, and Lisa Palley—

*who have always encouraged my ridiculous ideas, in exchange for my encouragement of **their** ridiculous ideas.*

OFFICIAL DISCLAIMER

This disclaimer was strongly recommended by our law firm—a firm which clearly has no sense of humor, but insists they're paid around $1200 an hour not to have a sense of humor, but rather to cover our rear ends. Perhaps. But they could still at least **smile** occasionally.

Here goes: This book is meant for **amusement** purposes only. The anti-social, illegal, and ridiculous actions and behaviors suggested in these pages are **not** intended to be taken seriously. If you're dense enough to actually **follow** any of the advice contained herein, **you're on your own,** pal. You can suffer the consequences all by yourself. In the county jail. Or worse. And we'll venture to say that'll be the **last** time you take one of **Bob Glickman's** books seriously.

—Publisher
&
Author

TABLE OF CONTENTS

PREFACE...*i*

A COMPILATION OF IDIOTS: WHO ARE
   THOSE GUYS?...*1*

INTRODUCTION *10*

THE 10 MOST COMMON DRIVING-RELATED
   QUESTIONS *11*

THE WORST REAL EXCUSES EVER GIVEN
   BY IDIOT DRIVERS *12*

CHAPTER ONE — *YOUR DRIVER'S LICENSE*...............*15*
Who Needs a License? People Who Cannot Get a License. What are the
Different Classes of Drivers? Possible Restrictions on your License. The
License Examination. The Issuing of the License. Fees for Licenses.
Providing Proof of Who You Are. Changing Your Name or Address. When
Must You Carry Your License? Your License Plate. Your Registration and
Title. Do you realize you're the only person who actually reads the table of
contents?

CHAPTER TWO — *YOU AND YOUR*
   DRIVING PRIVILEGE *25*
Drinking, Driving, and 'Rithmetic. Drugs. Falling Asleep at the Wheel. The
Point System. Driving School. License Penalties. Drivers' Records. In an
Accident. Accident Involving Unattended Vehicle. Safety in the Car. Driver's
Education Classes. Energy Conservation. It's a Rutabaga.

CHAPTER THREE — *SPECIAL DRIVING*
   SITUATIONS *37*
Road Construction. School Zones. School Buses. Emergency Vehicles.
Funeral Processions. Speed Bumps. Elderly Drivers. Rubbernecking.
Littering. Hitchhikers. Weapons and Driving. Defensive Driving. Emergency
Driving Techniques. Driving and Animals. Don't Sneeze Until We're Good
and Ready.

CHAPTER FOUR — *RULES OF THE ROAD* 47
Road Signs. Traffic Signals. Drivers' Signals. Speed Limit Regulations. Pavement Markings. Use of Lanes. Changing Lanes. Changing Clothes. Turns. U-Turns. The Three-Point Turn. Expressway Driving. Emergency Stopping. Passing. Night Driving. Following Distance. Stopping Distance. Railroad Crossings. Safety Belts. Child Restraint Devices. Parking. Parking on a Hill. Parallel Parking. Pulling Out, No Parking Zones. Parking by Disabled Permit. Toll Booths. Eating Cereal Without Milk.

CHAPTER FIVE — *YOUR VEHICLE* 79
Maximum Size of Vehicle. Mandatory Equipment. Optional Equipment. How to Handle a Vehicular Breakdown. Exhaust Requirements. Vehicle Inspection. Preventing Auto Theft. Carjacking. I'd Rather Put My Hand in a Stranger's Mouth.

CHAPTER SIX — *FOREIGN DRIVERS* 87
A Chapter of Their Own.

CHAPTER SEVEN — *SHARING THE ROAD WITH NON-VEHICULAR & SEMI-VEHICULAR BEINGS* 89
Pedestrians. Blind Pedestrians. Pedestrian Responsibilities. Equestrians. Skateboards, Joggers and Bikes. Bicycle Rider Responsibilities. Motorcycles. Recreational Vehicles and Campers. Airplanes. I Got Your Recreational Vehicle—Right Here.

CHAPTER EIGHT — *SAMPLE TEST QUESTIONS* 95

CONCLUSION 99

PREFACE

You, undoubtedly, are a good driver. You're careful, courteous, and committed to following the rules and regulations listed in your state's Driver's Handbook. In summary, driving for you is probably **boring as hell.** Meanwhile, the Idiot Drivers out there are having all the fun!

If only you could turn your experiences with Idiot Drivers into your **own** fun on the road.

Well now you can. We understand and sympathize with your total frustration behind the wheel, and have therefore dedicated this book to you, **The Good Driver,** for having to put up with the stupidity of those idiots you encounter on the road every day.

So stop **driving** yourself nuts, and come join us for a carload of laughs. Let's start by taking a closer look at a few of our favorite Idiot Drivers.

A COMPILATION OF IDIOTS

—WHO *ARE* THOSE GUYS?—

"*You Idiot!***"** Ah, yes...the most common words to cross the mind of a driver. A phrase that is muttered by even the sweetest, kindest people we know. Undoubtedly, even the Pope, when cut off in traffic, must think to himself, *You @*#!%* Idiot!*

With this in mind, we begin this tell-it-like-it-is "Driver's Guide" with a look at just **some** of the idiots we all encounter on our roadways. You've probably "run into" them a time or two....

• **The Soon-To-Be-Deceased Senior Citizen.** They've fallen and they can't get up—except to drive! These blue-haired bundles of joy have lost virtually all of their sensory perception, their judgement abilities, and their reflexes, not to mention their bladder control. What a mess. When you realize they have all this to contend with, you really can't blame them for driving like a crash dummy.

• **The Blinker Blockhead.** Driving down the road with his turn signal perpetually on, he's letting the world know he's going to turn. We just don't know if it's going to be this week.

• **The Terrible Tailgating Twit.** This guy isn't happy unless he's following you closely enough to use YOUR rear-view mirror to see if his teeth are clean. His brain is too small to comprehend that there's a danger in following you going 55 miles per hour at a distance of 13 inches. He makes you want to slam on your brakes just for the fun of it. But don't. His lack of intelligence is probably surpassed only by his lack of insurance.

• **The 7-Day-A-Week Sunday Driver.** Trudging along at 20 miles per hour, they've got no place to go and nothing to do. They have no life. They're clueless to the fact that there's a world trying to take place around them. These people have had their Cruise Control replaced with Snooze Control, and they've decided to spend their afternoon snoozing in front of **you.**

- **The Car Phone Prima Donna.** A driver should concentrate on just one thing when behind the wheel—the radio station he's listening to. Anything more can interrupt one's driving abilities, as evidenced by these idiots on their mobile phones. When you see them trying to drive and carry on a conversation simultaneously, it's pretty clear that the next number they'll be dialing is 911.

- **The Tourist From Hell.** They're so busy staring at, pointing at, and photographing every tourist attraction in your city, they forget that trivial little requisite to driving known as "paying attention." But that's OK, because tourist dollars go a long way in helping your city...helping your city rebuild the landmarks that the tourists crash into; helping tear up and reconstruct major roadways due to the hoards of tourists jamming them up; and helping promote your area to **more** tourists, so this vicious cycle will forever continue.

- **The Pea-Brained Left Lane Loser.** Surely life's most annoying driver, he enters the expressway, heads to the far left lane, and remains there, **forever.** Despite the fact that this lane is reserved for **passing only,** this idiot—through either sheer stubbornness or utter stupidity—refuses under any circumstances to get his butt out of the lane, thus fouling up traffic for miles. He is one of the main reasons drivers now carry guns.

- **The Green Light "Gotta Go!" Guy.** How lucky we are that this idiot exists, for he saves us **so** much time. When the traffic light turns green and he's behind us, he helps us out by furiously beeping his horn within 3/64 of a nanosecond. If you look closely in your rear-view mirror, you can actually see him frothing at the mouth, with his eyes spinning, as he launches into a tirade that can't be printed in this wholesome book.

• **The Instant Law-Abiding Citizen.** She's driving down the highway, blending smoothly with traffic at 62 mph, when suddenly, she slams on her brakes and slows to 30 mph. Something in the roadway? Not quite. She's spotted a cop on the side of the road, 450 yards away, writing some other schnook a ticket. Obviously, she's concerned that the cop will eye her specific car as traveling seven miles per hour over the speed limit, abandon writing the current ticket, jump in his car, race to catch up, and ticket **her** instead. We should be so lucky.

• **Foreigners.** Need we say more?

• **The Pompous Ass.** Wait at a red light? No way. Get stuck in a traffic jam? Don't be silly! He'll just take a little detour, into the emergency lane, over the median, and through a girl scout troop. It doesn't matter how. All that matters is that there's no way he's going to have to wait like—Gasp!—the rest of us drivers.

• **The High-Beamer.** He's either visually-challenged, or just plain arrogant, but this guy will not dim his high-beam headlights for anyone. You'll spot him either behind you, illuminating the inside of your car like an all-night grocery store, or driving toward you, burning his headlight pattern permanently into your retinas. Don't even **try** flashing your brights at him—he's not familiar with the term "bright." The High-Beamer causes perfectly rational people to slow down dramatically, forcing Mr. Bright to pass them, so they can then turn on **their** brights and blind **him.**

• **The Li'l Engine That Couldn't.** Everybody's vehicle breaks down **some**time. This guy's vehicle breaks down **every** time. Most often in the middle of the roadway. During rush hour. In 90° heat. His **vehicular** breakdown will often cause your **mental** breakdown. When you finally reach him, don't give him a disgusted look—give him some spare change. After one week, he'll have earned enough to buy a **real** vehicle.

• **The "Get Ready, Get Set...Wait!" Guy.** When the light turns from red to green, he turns from driver to dreamer. A slight tap

YOU CAN GO NOW... OR ARE YOU WAITING FOR **HIM** TO TURN GREEN?

on your horn will usually snap him back into reality. Yes, a slight tap from your bumper to his would be more fun, but he might not share in your enthusiasm.

- **The Mid-Light Crisis.** You're at the intersection, waiting to make a left turn, when the light turns yellow, and then red. You go. And that's fine, as long as you're the first or second car through the red light. For that matter, even the third car has been accepted in recent years. But now we've got these idiots who think it's OK to be the **fourth** car through. They're sadly mistaken. If pulled over, they'll tell the officer they thought the yellow light was longer. They no doubt spend their lives pretending things are longer than they actually are.

- **The 60 To Zero In 4.0 Lanes.** She's in the left lane of the busy roadway, when—with the immediacy seen only in cats darting from one room to another for no apparent reason—she zips across traffic to turn right at the intersection she's currently passing. That is, until she decides she doesn't feel like turning there after all, at which point she zips across traffic back to the left lane. It's best to give her a few square miles of personal zipping space.

- **The Litter Critter.** Here we have the guy who thinks of the roadway as one large garbage pail—and with him out there, who can argue? As you drive behind him, you'll see him tossing out everything from cigarette butts to crushed soda cans to grungy appliances. When he stops at a red light, go up and tell him you're Mother Nature's personal representative. Explain that she's really pissed, and that if one more piece of trash goes out his window, she'll personally see to it that a swarm of killer bees makes its permanent home in his pajama bottoms.

- **The Rubbernecking Bubba.** This is the same guy who **lives** for those cheesy "reality" crime and rescue tabloid TV shows. To satisfy his insatiable appetite for horror, perhaps we could create theme parks dedicated to blood and guts, nauseating tragedy, and hysterical family members. Nah...he'd still slow down for a chance to gawk at the real thing.

5

- **The Nonexistent Turn Signaler.** Clearly concerned about overusing his turn signals and having to buy new 45 cent bulbs, he opts to not use his blinkers at all. In fact, the first clue that he's changing lanes or turning in front of you is often the inflation of your airbag.

- **The Physics Failure.** Here we have the person who should have studied just a little harder in math and science class, as she consistently fails to judge the speed of oncoming traffic—say 45 mph—as she heads into the roadway at approximately **three** miles per hour. She provides you with an unplanned opportunity to test how effective your brakes really are. You'll know they're defective if you end up wearing her tailpipe home that night.

- **Red Roller, Red Roller.** She knows that making a right on red is legal. She just forgets that eensy-weensy detail about **STOPPING** first. You'll often meet her at an intersection as you follow the left turn signal, and she cuts you off from the opposite direction as she makes a "right on red" at 47 mph. And then, when you both slam on your brakes, she'll give you such a lethal look that you'll actually question whether it **was** your fault.

- **The Foreign Taxi Driver.** How confusing all of our traffic rules must be to those new to our country. For a graphic illustration of this phenomenon, simply follow a foreign taxi driver for six blocks, and see if you can keep count of the honking horns, piercing screams, and flying pedestrians.

- **The Super-Cool Hot Rod Bad Dude.** Whatever you do, **don't** accidentally look over at him at a red light. Because if your eyes meet his, when the light turns green, you've got yourself an all-out drag race. Luckily, the coolest of the cool often have their windows tinted solid black, so we can't even **see** how cool they are.

- **The Cowardly Driver.** The best place to spot her is on the merge ramp to the expressway—stopped cold. She isn't quite sure which cars to merge between, so she has come to a complete stop to try to decide. Thanks to her, the drivers behind her, whom she has now also forced to stop cold, will soon get to see how long it **really** takes their cars to go from 0 to 60.

6

- **The Mobile Smog Generator.** We've all seen them chugging along, converting each ounce of fuel into thirty cubic pounds of smog and filth. Their attitude: "Hey, Who really needs more than 10 feet of visibility anyway?" While many cars now come equipped with airbags, you may wish to opt for air **masks** that automatically drop from the car's ceiling when you're behind one of these fools.

- **The Chuck Yeager.** Zipping past cars, personally trying to break the sound barrier, he doesn't let little things like **traffic** get in his way. After all, he's got important business to attend to— getting to the video arcade for another night of intense intellectual challenge. "Hey, man, why do you think the speedometer goes up to 120 mph?"

- **The Stick Shift Virgin.** They sit in front of you **looking** like a normal car. But when they start to go, they suddenly stop. And go. And stop. And go. And stop. Hey—what better place to learn to drive a stick shift than a busy thoroughfare?

- **The Scholarly Airhead.** This idiot can be seen doing everything from reading the *Wall Street Journal* while driving to curling her hair while driving. If the activity takes at least 95% of her concentration off the road, you'll find her engrossed in it. Unfortunately, she's also one of those people who can't walk and chew gum at the same time.

- **The Classic Redneck.** You can often drive right **under** his truck, as it is modified to sit at least fifteen feet off the ground. The higher the struts, the more masculine the driver is (though he can't actually **spell** words as big as "masculine"). To identify the Classic Redneck, look for a gun rack, a Confederate flag, and an unmistakable look of stupidity on the driver's face.

- **The Slo-Mo Schmo.** Here we have a Sunday Driver who has discovered the freeway. His thought process must go something like this: "What a pleasant roadway this is—not a single traffic light or stop sign to slow me down—I can maintain a nice, steady 23 miles per hour without bothering anyone." They just turn up their radio so they don't hear the sounds of screeching tires and crunching metal behind them.

• **The Lost Soul.** Driving slowly down the road, these people can be seen spinning their heads like they're possessed, frantically looking for an address or street that is, in fact, forty miles away. A woman will eventually stop for directions. A man, however, as dictated by his genes, is forbidden to ask directions. He will continue driving until he finds his way back to civilization. Even if it takes years.

• **The Anti-Merge.** He's driving on the highway. You're about to **enter** the highway. Planning to merge in front of him? Think again. If necessary, he'll speed up to 120 miles per hour to prevent your getting in. It's best to let him have his way. It's probably the only thing in life he'll ever succeed at.

• **The Two-Laner.** If there are two lanes on the road headed in the same direction, you can count on her to be right between 'em. It never occurs to her there might be other drivers behind her who need one of those lanes to pass her. No, she's in her own little world, conveniently using the painted line as a centering guide.

• **The "Weaving is Believing" Guy.** He creeps a little into your lane, and then back into his. He creeps into the next lane, and back into his. Basically, he's a creep. You see, he's not **changing** lanes—he's just **looking** like he's about to change lanes...just enough to give your adrenal glands a nice workout.

• **The Pigheaded Left-Turning Thrill Seeker.** She's **going** to make her left turn. Out of a side street or driveway, blocking five lanes of traffic, she's **going** to make her left turn. Try suggesting she make a right turn and then a U-turn like a sensible driver. Too late. She's now blocking **all** lanes of traffic in both directions. She's **going** to make her left turn.

• **The Boom Box on Wheels.** You will usually **hear** him before you see him, as the car's stereo system is powerful enough for the entire state of Texas. The bass from the music (the term "music" is used very loosely here) will just perceptibly interrupt the rhythm of your heart. Have some fun. As he pulls beside you, motion for him to crank the music up **louder.** This will

8

freak him out. His sense of power will suddenly come into question, and he'll feel that his woofer isn't big enough after all.

• **The Lickety-Splat.** Here we have the motorcyclist who wants his two-wheeled investment to pay off, and therefore races between lanes and cars at about Mach II faster than the vehicles he's passing. While you may have a sick little fantasy of opening your car door to discourage this maneuver, keep it to yourself. These guys are usually "taken care of" by some unsuspecting motorist who's simply in the process of changing lanes. Lickety-Splat.

• **The One For The Road.** The idiot of all idiots—the drunk driver. Just try telling him he's not up to driving a car. He'll tell you he's feeling good enough to pilot the Space Shuttle. Actually, that wouldn't be such a bad idea. At least he'd be off the road.

Sometimes you'll be lucky enough to spot interaction between two or more of the above. This "Ballet of Idiots" can be quite enjoyable to watch, such as when a Chuck Yeager zips by you, and then encounters a Pea-Brained Left Lane Loser. **This** is driving at its very best.

Now that you've acquainted yourself with many of the idiots on the roadway, it's **your** turn to have the fun. It's time to explore the world of Idiot Drivers!

INTRODUCTION

Driving has changed a lot over the years. Remember when the main mode of transportation was horse and buggy? Of course you don't. You'd be dead by now. But if you **did** remember that time, you'd know that drivers were both cautious and polite back then—they didn't even carry Uzi's.

Luckily, things are different today. Driving nowadays can be downright fun!

First of all, forget about that ridiculous "official" driver's handbook that you pick up at your local Department of Motor Vehicles office after waiting in line for seven hours behind some big smelly guy. Following those rules can put you to sleep faster than a late-night TV real estate infomercial.

You want to enjoy yourself on the road, and that's what this book is all about. Just think of this as a fun guide to a wild ride.

THE 10 MOST COMMON DRIVING-RELATED QUESTIONS

- Where'd ya learn to drive?

- Why did the chicken cross the road?

- Is that a stick shift, or are you just happy to see me?

- Do ya want fries with that?

- Have you gained weight, or did your airbag just inflate?

- Are we there yet?

- If you crash into another car on purpose, is it still called an accident?

- Do you know how fast you were going?

- Well, would you consider locking all four doors constitutes safe sex?

- What pump you at? (Formerly "Would you like me to check under the hood for you, ma'am?")

These questions, along with many others, will not be answered in this book.

THE WORST **REAL** EXCUSES EVER GIVEN BY IDIOT DRIVERS

It's one of life's most challenging moments—what to say after you're caught committing a driving infraction or causing an accident.

Take, for example, the San Francisco man who was pulled over for driving by himself in the car-pool lane. He actually told the cop that his dog, who sat next to him on the front seat, should be considered a passenger. Why? The driver, who claimed to be partially blind, said his dog assisted him by barking when cars were approaching.

With that **TRUE** story serving as a fair warning, let's delve deep into the crusty inner workings of the Idiot Driver's mind, and take a look at some other **REAL-LIFE** excuses taken from **ACTUAL** accident reports....

- "The guy was all over the road. I had to swerve a number of times before I hit him."
- "I don't know what happened because I was thrown from my car as it left the road. I was later found in a ditch by some stray cows."
- "The telephone pole was approaching fast. I was attempting to swerve out of its path when it struck my front end."
- "My car was legally parked as it backed into the other vehicle."
- "I was sure that the old fellow would never make it to the other side of the road when I struck him."
- "Coming home I drove into the wrong driveway and collided with a tree I don't have."
- "I thought my window was down but found out it was up when I put my head through it."
- "The pedestrian hit me and went under my car."

- "In my attempt to kill a fly, I drove into a telephone pole."
- "I was on my way to the doctor's with rear end trouble when my universal joint gave way causing me to have an accident."
- "The pedestrian had no idea what direction to go, so I ran over him."
- "As I approached the intersection, a stop sign suddenly appeared in a place where no stop sign had ever appeared before and I was unable to stop in time."
- "The other car collided with mine without giving any warning of its intentions."
- "The truck carelessly backed through my windshield into my wife's face."
- "To avoid hitting the bumper of the car in front, I struck the pedestrian."
- "An invisible car came out of nowhere, struck my vehicle, and vanished."
- "The indirect cause of this accident was a little guy in a small car with a big mouth."

Now that you better understand the mind of the Idiot Driver we're dealing with, you should proceed with extreme caution.

CHAPTER ONE

YOUR DRIVER'S LICENSE

- **Do I Need a License?**
- **How Do I Obtain a License?**
- **How Do I *Spell* the word License?**
- **Why Am I Asking Myself These Inane Questions?**

The driver's license is a small card that signifies you have completed the prerequisites necessary to operate a vehicle on public roadways. It also shows people what you look like when you're ready to throw up.

WHO NEEDS A LICENSE?

- You **Don't** need a License if:
  - A) You're driving an agricultural vehicle.
  - B) You're driving a road maintenance vehicle.
  - C) You're a foreigner—it wouldn't make any difference.

- You **Do** need a License if:
  - A) You plan to drive a motor vehicle for personal use.
  - B) You plan to get a job which involves driving a motor vehicle.
  - C) You plan to buy a *Playboy* magazine at Quik-Mart and you look fifteen.

PEOPLE WHO CANNOT GET A LICENSE

A) Any person whose license has been suspended or revoked.

B) Any person who is considered a hazard to public safety.

C) Any person who has bought tickets to a Pia Zadora concert.

WHAT ARE THE DIFFERENT CLASSES OF DRIVERS?

– Junior Operators.

Typically, teenagers learning how to drive. This permit is sometimes called a **Restricted** License, because your driving time is often restricted to the hours when your parents are asleep.

– Operators.

Those persons driving passenger cars and trucks, or those persons working for the phone company.

– Chauffeurs, Bus Drivers, and Truck Drivers.

Men named James, Ralph, and Mack, respectively.

POSSIBLE RESTRICTIONS ON YOUR LICENSE

- Drive only during daylight.
- Drive only between the hours of 3 a.m. and 4 a.m., **in your own driveway.**
- Must wear corrective lenses.
- Must **not** wear corrective lenses (unless they're tinted fuchsia).
- Must not wear plaids and stripes together.
- Must wear a bag over face or have heavily tinted windows.
- If legally blind, must have a Seeing Eye dog next to driver at all times.

THE LICENSE EXAMINATION

In order to obtain your driver's license, you will need to take the standard License Exam. This consists of various tests, all of which must be passed or faked to obtain a license. These include:

- Vision Test
- Hearing Test
- Oral Test (outlawed in most states)
- Written Test
- Stress Test
- Driving Test
- SAT Test
- Rorshach Test
- Pregnancy Test

You must take your exam at an official driver's license office. It's a good indication that you're at a bogus office if the examiner asks you to turn your head and cough. Especially if you're a woman.

Many license bureaus offer you the opportunity to make an appointment in advance, rather than having to wait in line. However, recent studies have shown that the time spent on the phone trying to make an appointment, and either receiving a busy signal, being put on hold, or trying to explain to the office employee "what an appointment is," typically takes longer than just showing up without an appointment.

Of course, you can always make your appointment **in person.** Simply go to the license office, stand in line behind 54 people for two hours, and make your appointment. Then go back at your appointed time and get in line behind the same 54 people.

– The Written Test. This will measure either your knowledge of the driving rules, or your ability to cheat in a large room full of unsupervised people taking the same identical test. In recent years, however, some states have made cheating more dif-

18

ficult by requiring you to answer essay questions written in foreign languages.

(Sample questions from the Written Test can be found at the end of this book.)

– **The Driving Test.** This requires you to perform a series of driving maneuvers, while a sweaty, grotesque examiner from the Department of Motor Vehicles sits in your car. The sole purpose of this test is to make you even more nervous than you would normally be during the parallel parking procedure.

To represent actual driving scenarios, you may also be asked to:

- Start the car.
- Go.
- Stop.
- Change the radio station while driving.
- Change a tire on a busy freeway.
- Give another driver the finger while making a right turn.
- Eat a burger and fries, and balance a large Coke, while braking.
- Sneeze while maintaining complete control of the car.
- Turn your head ninety degrees to the left to check out a hot babe or hunk, without rear-ending the car in front of you.
- Squash a flying insect in the car without becoming the star of a Driver's Ed "Wrecks From Hell" film.

Of course, examiners have the option of waiving all of the above exercises, provided you cart them around town to run their errands. Also, it is best to use an old car during the test, as the examiner will sometimes be eating an overflowing meatball sub during the driving test.

– **The Vision Test.** This helps the state determine whether your eyesight is sharp enough to operate a vehicle. They do this by showing you a picture of Ernest Borgnine, naked. If you puke, you pass.

– The Hearing Test. This is given to make sure your hearing is adequate, so you would be able to hear any warning sounds such as a car horn or siren. If you have trouble hearing the examiner's instructions, they will call out Earl, who will stand behind you, cup his hands around his mouth, and make the sound of a siren in your ear. If you don't hear Earl, you don't get a license.

THE ISSUING OF THE LICENSE

Once you satisfactorily complete all of the tests, your photograph will be taken for your license.

Note: If you slip the person behind the counter a few bucks, he or she will sometimes pose **with** you in the photograph.

Cardboard cut-outs of celebrities are also available in some locations.

Of course, no matter what you do to look good for your driver's license photo, you will always end up looking like you were having a near-death experience when the shot was taken.

After your photograph, you will be asked if you would like to donate any of your organs. (You need not actually **donate** them until some time in the future.)

Of course, if you have an old Wurlitzer that you no longer use, by all means bring it in—the DMV might give you preferential treatment when you renew your license, and next time, you'll only have to wait in line for **three** hours.

FEES FOR LICENSES

At the time your license is issued, you will also be responsible for paying all applicable fees, as well as some nonapplicable fees.

- Initial License...$ 20.00
- License Renewal 200.00

WILL A MOUTH ORGAN DO?

SIGN UP HERE TO BE AN ORGAN DONOR

Additional charges for special services:

- Changing date of birth to make you older.......................$ 5.00
- Changing date of birth to make you younger....................45.00
- Creating a boudoir setting for your photograph................70.00
- Making your license "scratch and sniff".........................95.00

PROVIDING PROOF OF WHO YOU ARE

To obtain a license, you must provide positive identification of who you are. This can include:

A) Birth Certificate.

B) Voter Registration Card.

C) Telling the person behind the counter something **only you** would know.

CHANGING YOUR NAME OR ADDRESS

If you change your name or address, you must bring official documentation to the license office to certify these modifications. If you change your name **and** your address, you should have a special agent take care of that, as you're obviously in the Federal Witness Protection Program.

WHEN MUST YOU CARRY YOUR LICENSE?

When driving, you must **always** carry your license, though not necessarily in your hand. While you must show it to any law enforcement officer who asks to see it, you may use your thumb to cover the hideous photo.

YOUR LICENSE PLATE

Your car must have a valid license plate whenever it is driven on public roads. In most states, your license plate will contain a combination of numbers and letters, such as

"2784KGM". Less populous states (i.e. New Hampshire) are able to have more simplified license plate combinations, such as "4".

If you prefer to operate your vehicle without incurring the cost of a license plate, you can always take a piece of cardboard, and in your sloppiest handwriting, scrawl the words "Lost Tag." Granted, you have to be a pretty disorganized person for anyone to believe you really lost a piece of metal that's screwed onto your car, but the sham sometimes actually works.

A variation of this idea is to write the words "Stolen Tag" on a piece of cardboard. This also helps to discourage thieves from stealing your car. No car thief wants to be driving down the road in a car with the word "stolen" on it.

For an extra charge, you can get a "vanity" or "customized" license plate, where the letter or number combination is chosen by you. Each state carefully monitors this option to prevent the display of any language or message it deems to be offensive, such as "IM A HO", "DMV SUCKS", or "BITE ME". Most states also won't allow customized plates that they consider confusing, such as the letter combination "LOST TAG".

DIPLOMATIC PLATES

These special plates provide foreign diplomats with complete, unbridled immunity. When a cop pulls one of these guys over for crashing his car through a crowded mall and running over screaming shoppers, he just smiles, points to his diplomatic plate, and says, "I'm sure you won't mind cleaning up this little mess—I'm late for cocktails. See ya."

YOUR REGISTRATION AND TITLE

– **Registration.** This is the small piece of paper the state gives you in exchange for about a month's salary. It registers your car with the state, so if you ever do anything wrong, the state knows exactly where to find you.

– Title. Your title is "Driver." Some states allow special titles such as "Hot Rod" or "Speed Demon." Other states permit such classic titles as "An Old Man and the Sea" or "A Tale of Two Cities." For **your** state's rules, call your particular Department of Motor Vehicles, listen to the constant busy signal, and once again hang up in frustration.

CHAPTER TWO

YOU AND YOUR DRIVING PRIVILEGE

Driving is a privilege—not a right. On the other hand, picking your nose at a red light is a **right**. (And, for that matter, a privilege.)

Driving is also a responsibility. When you're behind the wheel of a car, make sure the wheel of the car is in front of **you**. If it's not, then you're facing the wrong way.

It is vital you understand that driving can be a very dangerous activity. **Studies show driving to be more hazardous than:**

• Flying in an airplane.
• Riding a train.
• Running with a pair of scissors.
• Teasing a pit bull.
• Playing Russian roulette.
• Bungee jumping off a card table.
• Eating tuna salad that hasn't been refrigerated for four days.
• Setting off fireworks in your shorts.

However, by being a safety-conscious driver, or at least by being a **conscious** driver, you can minimize your risk of serious death.

DRINKING, DRIVING, AND 'RITHMETIC

Drinking alcohol and then attempting to drive is a deadly combination. It has been shown repeatedly that drinking alcohol significantly slows our reaction time and affects our judgment.

For example, driving after a few drinks has been known to cause drivers to incessantly search their car radio until finding a song by Leon Redbone. Such an act obviously takes one's concentration off the road. It also supports the theory of impaired judgment.

So how many alcoholic beverages are safe to consume before driving? For that matter, How many alcoholics does it take to screw in a light bulb? Ignoring the latter question, the answer to the first question depends on a number of factors:

- Your body weight.
- The food content in your stomach.
- Your sex.
- Your lack of sex.
- Your fly is open.
- How quickly you consumed the drinks.
- Whether you used a straw.
- The last time you thought about Abe Vigoda.

Statistics show that even <u>one drink</u> can impair a driver's abilities. Even if it's just a Sprite.

Drunk driving is one offense that even disgusts other idiot drivers. And idiot drivers, as a whole, are not easy to disgust.

DRUGS

Certain drugs can also seriously affect your driving skills, and should be avoided when you're behind the wheel. You must be cautious with any of the following....

– **Over-the-counter drugs.** These can include products such as cold medicines, which can cause severe drowsiness, and can make you fall asleep at the wheel. On the up side, when you slam into that oak tree at 62 miles per hour, your nasal passages will be nice and clear, allowing you to smell the fumes from the ruptured gas tank, which in turn will wake you for an attempted escape.

– **Prescription drugs.** These often have side effects which can pose a danger while driving. Since pharmacists can't really read the gibberish your doctor scribbles on the prescription pad, you may never receive appropriate warnings related to the drugs. If you must drive, turn on your flashers, lean on your horn, and keep your airbag inflated.

– **Illegal drugs.** These should be avoided even when you're not driving. This is because they will alter your mind to such a degree that you may **think** you're driving, and you suddenly find yourself trying to merge into highway traffic without a vehicle, and completely naked.

FALLING ASLEEP AT THE WHEEL

Though the notion of falling asleep while driving seems like something that couldn't happen to you, the brain has a way of denying its true degree of exhaustion. While your head repeatedly falls toward your lap, your brain happily jerks you back to attention, confident that you can nevertheless handle a 3000-pound vehicle barreling along at 85 miles per hour.

As a general rule, you should pull over the moment you start dreaming that you missed class all semester and now have to take the final exam.

THE POINT SYSTEM

Each state's DMV has what's called the **Point System.** When you are found guilty of a driving violation, points will be assessed against your license.

If you accumulate enough points over a certain period of time, you will be eligible to buy any of the gifts on display, such as the La-Z-Boy Recliner, the lifetime supply of Rice-A-Roni, or any other product with two hyphens. And you can take the rest on a gift certificate.

DRIVING SCHOOL

To keep points off your record after a driving infraction, most states allow you to attend Driving School. In this special school, instructors attempt to frighten you into better driving techniques by showing you films of car crash scenes and emergency rescue procedures. It's very similar to sitting back and watching some of those "real-life" TV shows at night, or even being treated to an adventure movie with lots of car chase scenes. On the down side, you must bring your own popcorn.

LICENSE PENALTIES

– **Suspension.** For certain driving violations, your license may be temporarily taken away, or suspended. These violations vary from state to state.

- Most Strict. Maryland—where you can temporarily lose your license for sneezing with your window open.

- Most Lenient. Oklahoma—where you can stop your automobile right in the middle of the highway, climb on the roof of the car naked, and sing "I've Got a Lovely Bunch of Coconuts."

– **Revocation.** Your license can be taken away permanently, or revoked, for serious driving errors, including but not limited to:

- Applying make-up in the rear-view mirror while driving to work.

- Driving with bald tires.

- Driving with bald head (reflection of the sun can blind other drivers).

- Driving a traffic judge crazy with stupid excuses.
- Driving for more than seventeen blocks with your left blinker on.

  – Public Hanging. This is reserved for the most severe vehicular illegalities, such as:

- Seeing how fast your motor vehicle can actually go, in a school zone.
- Being involved in a traffic accident while wearing dirty underwear. (Your mother warned you about that one.)
- Parking in a policeman's spot at the local donut shop.

Driving with a suspended license is considered a felony in most states, and is punishable by up to ten years locked in a very small room with Tommy Tune. ("Would you **stop** with the **dancing** already!")

If you are caught driving after your license has been permanently revoked, your license will be suspended for an additional three months after your death.

DRIVERS' RECORDS

Drivers' records are generally kept for seven years. You may, therefore, now toss out any L.P.'s by KC & The Sunshine Band.

IN AN ACCIDENT

Your first responsibility after being involved in an accident is to make sure the other party isn't injured. If they are okay, you may then take out your anger by injuring them.

Also, **do not** move your car. Do not move your bowels. Do not pass Go and do not collect 200 dollars.

After calling the police, you should exchange information with the other driver. This should include:

- Your name and address.
- Your insurance company.
- Your zodiac sign.
- What you like to do on a first date.
- Your kinkiest sexual experience.
- Your alternate uses for mayonnaise.
- Your favorite *I Love Lucy* episode.

ACCIDENT INVOLVING UNATTENDED VEHICLE

If you hit an unattended vehicle, look for any witnesses. If there are none, consider yourself lucky and quickly get the hell out of there.

Be aware, however, that leaving the scene of any accident is illegal. Of course, if a tree falls in the forest and nobody's around to hear it, the tree can't be called in for questioning.

SAFETY IN THE CAR

There are many steps you can take to make your time in the car as safe as possible. These include:

- When driving, always wear a safety belt.
- When having sex in the car, always wear a condom.
- When having oral sex while driving, try not to smile too big.
- Buy a car with a driver-side airbag. This was designed for those times when safety is a prime concern, but you really don't care all that much about the person in the passenger seat.
- When at the wheel, concentrate on the road and limit your conversations with passengers. If you talk to yourself when driving alone, at least get a fake car phone to minimize your chance of being pointed out as some kind of loon.

- When stopping at a red light in a bad part of town, immediately turn on your windshield washer and wipers, thereby eliminating the need for "personal" service.
- Always remember that nine out of every ten drivers have absolutely no idea where they're going or why.

DRIVER'S EDUCATION CLASSES

It is a good idea to take a Driver's Ed course when learning how to drive. Often part of the high school curricula, this elective class can get you out of a **real** class, such as Trigonometry. Ask any adult how many hours per week they spend driving versus how many hours they spend doing Trigonometry. The young person who cares about his or her future will choose Driver's Ed.

ENERGY CONSERVATION

As a responsible driver, you should try to conserve fuel whenever possible. The following tips will help you to save energy and make our environment healthier for Spotted Owls everywhere.

- Do not leave your engine running for more than 60 seconds if you're not moving.
- Avoid jackrabbit starts, unless, of course, you happen to be a jackrabbit.
- Drive at moderate speeds, especially when there's a cop right behind you.
- Drive in a steady manner. Fast acceleration and sudden braking not only make you lose fuel economy—they can also make your passengers lose their lunch.
- Lighten the load. Less weight in the car means better gas mileage. In other words, go on a diet.

- Car-Pool—A terrific fuel saver, car-pooling consists of sharing a ride to a common destination with one or more persons whom, under any other circumstances, you would never actually **want** to be in the same car with.

THE FLAGMAN

REALITY

YOUR IMAGINATION

CHAPTER THREE

SPECIAL DRIVING SITUATIONS

ROAD CONSTRUCTION

Motor vehicles can be a serious hazard to road construction or maintenance personnel. Road work can also endanger the driver. To control the traffic flow in these areas, several methods are employed.

- **Signs.** These are put up to make you aware of nearby construction. There's really no need to change your speed or driving habits here.

- **Reduced Speed Limits.** To minimize possible dangers, speed limits are often reduced. There's really no need to change your speed or driving habits here.

- **Flagpersons.** For massive road work, the DMV hires people with no friends to wave flags to slow you down or stop you. There's really no need to change your speed or driving habits here.

- **Death Mazes.** Occasionally, road crews find it necessary to re-route vehicles to the opposite side of the street, across other traffic, between barricades, over the river and through the woods, to God-only-knows we go. There's really no need to change your speed or driving habits here.

Note: When orange cones are set up in a long row to close a lane, you may **not** test your skill as a "slalom course" driver.

As you drive through areas of road construction, keep in mind that you are permitted to steal only one barricade with a blinking light in the course of your lifetime. Most people take advantage of this opportunity during their college years, putting it in their dorm room for decoration.

You are **not** allowed to take one of the large electronic flashing information or arrow panels home, unless you're having a party and need it to direct guests to your house. As for bringing home flagpersons, the rules differ from state to state. But in all honesty, it's a waste of time—these people have no friends for a reason.

SCHOOL ZONES

On school days, students are no longer the only people who must suffer. Drivers are now required to slow down to a virtual stop within approximately a 40-mile radius of any school. In most states, this school zone even applies to high schools. However, by putting Darwin's theory to use, you can maintain your normal speed around high schools, and the smarter kids **will** survive.

SCHOOL BUSES

Drivers must follow a few special rules when sharing the road with school buses.

- If a school bus in front of you flashes its red lights and puts out its "Stop" signs, you must stop. However, you **may** rev up your engine to frighten the kids.

- If a student gives you the finger, you are permitted to give him the finger in return, provided the vehicle is not a church bus.

- If you are the victim of one or more spitballs, you may wish to refer to the "How To Use Weapons While Driving" section later in this handbook.

EMERGENCY VEHICLES

You must yield to any emergency vehicle that is using its siren, **if** you can hear that siren over your: 1) engine; 2) mobile phone; 3) 100-watt stereo system; & 4) loud passengers.

If you spot an emergency vehicle coming up behind you with flashing lights, you should pull over, let it pass you, and then quickly pull behind it and let it clear the traffic for you.

FUNERAL PROCESSIONS

Drivers must yield the right-of-way to any funeral procession. If you wish, you may join the procession, but only if you turn on your headlights, put on dark sunglasses, and tell the family it was a lovely service. It would also be appropriate to bring a covered dish.

SPEED BUMPS

Speed bumps are designed to slow down drivers and to ruin your car's alignment. They began as mild pavement elevations in a few private parking lots, and today have grown into 10-inch high mounds multiplying exponentially throughout the industrialized world. This proliferation of speed bumps has provoked several important questions.

Q: What's the best way to deal with speed bumps?

A: Go **around** them, even if you have to drive on the grass or into oncoming traffic.

Q: What if I can't avoid the bump?

A: Go over it **very quickly.** Not only will this cause your car to sway less violently—it will also show the people who decided to install the bump that it's not working.

Q: What if my car isn't powerful enough to get over the speed bump?

A: Trade in your Hyundai for a real car.

Q: What does **Proliferation** mean?

A: We think it has something to do with rabbits.

GRIDLOCK

Gridlock is the vehicular equivalent of constipation. As much as you really want to get things moving, you're stuck. Caused by heavy traffic intersecting at major crossroads, gridlock brings all movement on the roadway to a grinding halt, and is relieved only when traffic lightens up, usually around 3 a.m.

ELDERLY DRIVERS (A.k.a. South Floridians)

Elderly citizens have special needs and concerns when behind the wheel. Being aware of their unique situation can help you more effectively deal with these crotchety old bags.

- **Seeing Over the Dashboard.** If you spot a seemingly-empty car driving down the road, look for knuckles on the steering wheel. This is an elderly driver. Or Danny DeVito. If you stop next to them at a red light, be polite, offer them some pillows or phone books, and be on your way.

- **Traveling Under 25 mph on the Expressway.** A slower rate of speed is generally equated with safer driving. However, this rule does not apply to the expressway, where older drivers are often seen only as a blur as we zip by them. When you spot such a driver, one way to help is to slowly pull right up behind them, and match their speed exactly, until the two cars are touching. Then **push** them up to expressway speed.

- **Ignoring Lanes, Signs, and Signals.** Older drivers have diminished sight and hearing capabilities, as well as slower reaction time. These factors combine to produce one hell of an abominable driver. Your best bet is to stay home where it's safe. (Just hope they don't crash through your living room wall.)

It is sometimes hard to determine at what point you should relinquish your license. As a general guide, you know you're getting too old to drive when....

41

- You only know to stop when the cars around you stop.
- Your great-great-grandson is teaching **his** son to drive.
- Your first license was made of mortar.
- You have to keep repeating: Right is gas. Left is brake.
- Your pants come up higher than the steering wheel.

RUBBERNECKING

The practice of rubbernecking began in California, where the early pioneers would be riding their horses, and would stop to look at a cactus for an hour for absolutely no reason. Then they'd move on.

The tradition continues today, but now involves motor vehicles and the entire nation. Until the fascination with a fender-bender or a stalled car ends, there seems little we can do to avoid such delays.

However, scientists are working on one possible solution: Having every motorist keep a big sign in their car which can be pulled out if they're ever stopped on the side of the road. It would simply say, "What the hell are **you** looking at?"

LITTERING

Littering, or throwing trash from your vehicle, is illegal, immoral, and disgusting. Of course, if you don't have a little trash container in your car, what else are you going to do with your garbage?

If you **are** going to litter, at least be a good citizen and throw your garbage out the window once you've already pulled into your own driveway.

HITCHHIKERS

The practice of picking up hitchhikers is against the law in most areas, due to the extreme embarrassment associated with letting a stranger see how messy your car is.

THE LIZZIE BORDEN AXIOM:
NEVER PICK UP A HITCHHIKER
CARRYING AN AXE

There is also some possibility of danger. Therefore, if you are driving in an area where hitchhiking is legal, and you feel compelled to pick someone up, beat them at their own game. When you stop, hand them your money and your keys, and let them take **you** for a ride.

WEAPONS AND DRIVING

Just as you like to keep your vehicle in good condition, weapons should also be well-maintained and checked frequently. Several tips should be kept in mind when combining weapons and driving.

- When shooting at a slow driver, **don't** shoot out his tires. This will only slow him down more.

- When discharging a firearm while driving, remember to open your window fully and prepare for a sudden recoil. Nothing is more uncomfortable than having your arm thrown back against the window frame unexpectedly.

- Try to avoid unconventional weapons. For example, unless you drive a convertible, it can very difficult to maneuver a bow and arrow.

DEFENSIVE DRIVING

One of the best ways to prevent problems on the road is to be a defensive driver. Besides automatic weapons, your car should have a bullet-proof windshield and a remotely-operated white surrender flag.

Defensive driving also means being prepared for any potential problems. For instance, if you see a ball roll into the street from between two parked cars, chances are that a child (or a parent with the **intelligence** of a child) is going to be running out after it. Yes, you must yield the right-of-way.

While defensive driving steps are common sense for some drivers, many people behind the wheel are completely ignorant of what defensive driving is all about. You know you're in the car with one of these drivers if you find yourself in the passenger

44

seat continually pushing down on an imaginary brake pedal.

EMERGENCY DRIVING TECHNIQUES

A prepared driver is always ready to handle emergencies. Below are some possible emergency situations and how to handle them.

- **Skidding.** Various conditions or actions can make your vehicle begin to skid. When this happens, you should let your foot off the gas and turn in the direction you wish to go.

  Of course, the popular misconception is to steer **into** the skid. In other words, if you're skidding towards oncoming cars, go ahead and steer right into them. This false information was created decades ago by a disgruntled and sadistic DMV employee. It will only plow you head-on into the oncoming traffic. (The former employee now lives in a room with padded walls.)

- **Sudden Reduced Visibility.** This can occur when heavy rain or thick fog quickly moves in, or when a passenger puts his or her hands over your eyes. Your best bet is to slam on your brakes, and then refer to the above paragraph on "Skidding."

- **Vehicle Goes Under Water.** Experts tell you not to panic if your car plunges into deep water. That's good advice. In fact, before trying to escape, you should play a couple rounds of cards, catch up on your reading, and see how many of the fishes swimming by you can identify.

- **Running Out Of Gas.** While not technically an emergency, this driving problem can be one of the most severe, in that you must face the embarrassment of walking back to your car with a gas can in hand. This can result in life-long psychological damage. It's therefore best to fill up every time you pass a gas station.

- **Brake Failure.** You need not worry about this problem unless you're an actor. Brake failure only happens on TV.

DRIVING AND ANIMALS

In every state except Kansas, it is unlawful for an animal to drive a motor vehicle. Many of the dead animals you see on the side of the road were "just out for a spin."

On the other hand, it **is** legal to transport animals such as dogs in the back of a pickup truck, provided the driver is an unsympathetic bonehead who doesn't care that the dog is trying to hang on for dear life.

Also be aware that animals will sometimes, without warning, walk into the path of your vehicle. This is because they don't understand the concept of fuel injection, or they **do** understand it and they're suicidal. Either way, you are required to yield the right-of-way to any animal. Except a possum.

CHAPTER FOUR

RULES OF THE ROAD

L earning the rules of the road is a necessity for the pleasurable operation of your vehicle. Otherwise, you'll drive like a Pakistani immigrant who's had his U.S. taxi license for three hours.

By knowing what to do, when to do it, where to do it, why to do it, how much to do, and whom you should do it to, you'll be well on your way to driving bliss.

ROAD SIGNS

Road signs help direct you as a driver. They are distinguishable by shape and color, as well as smell.

While most road signs are easily readable, the comprehension of **expressway** signage usually requires several years of speed reading courses.

For your everyday driving, you should be familiar with all of the following road signs, and be able to recognize them even when the top bolt is missing and the sign is hanging upside-down.

On the following pages, you will find street signs and their meanings. You must memorize them, or keep these pages taped to your dashboard at all times.

Your City Is Too Cheap To Fix This Street

Caution: Watch for School Children

Geraldo Rivera Ahead

Caution: Watch for Pedophiles

Derived from a combination of "No
Outhouse" and "No Toilet" meaning:
Don't stop here. Go Away.

Man On Tightrope Ahead

Happy Deer Crossing

Elderly Pedestrian Crossing

Bear Crossing

Bowling Pedestrian Crossing

Shelley Winters Crossing

Religious Intersection Ahead

Trucks On Triangular Blocks Ahead

Slippery When Wet

Extremely Slippery When Wet

**You May Have Trouble
Getting Off Roadway**

**You May Have Trouble
Getting Off**

Impotence Ahead

Traffic Goes Both Ways;
Bisexuals Welcome

Severe Impotence Ahead

If you're under 12' - 6",
You May Not Go On This Ride

No Impotence Ahead

Narrow Bridge:
There's not much you can do to prepare
for this, except maybe have your
passengers take a deep breath.

51

Stop Sign
You must come to a complete
stop, which today is defined as
slowing down to around 20 mph.

Yield Sign
Proceed as normal,
making *others* yield

Four Way Stop
If you arrive at a 4-way stop at the same
time as another car, yield to the car on
the right. Therefore, according to the
law, if four cars arrive at the intersection
at the exact same time, you'll either:
A) Have a 4-car accident; or
B) Be stranded at the intersection
for the rest of your natural life.

**Steer Around Pregnant
Woman In Roadway**

**While Passing, Smile
Politely And Thank Those In
Neighboring Vehicles**

Speed Limit Sign

**Center Lane Reserved For
Square Dancing**

Dyslexic Speed Limit Sign

If you collide with a vehicle displaying these signs, you'll never have to worry about traffic rules again.

You Know You're
In Trouble If The Top
Of The Sign Is Missing

Left Lane *Must* Turn Left.
Don't even *think* about not turning
left. How dare the concept even
enter your mind. In fact, you either
turn left, or you'll be shot. So *there*!

Traffic Must Flow In This Direction

Why Be Normal

Translation: You Are An Idiot

Don't Do Nothing

No Drawing Pictures Of Trucks

Stop Looking Up

You Are Running Late For A Very Important Meeting

TRAFFIC SIGNALS

These are the electronic lights at intersections that tend to be red no matter which direction you approach from. Of course, in some cities, the signals on each block are timed via computer, so that every light you hit will **definitely** be red.

You must obey these signals to keep traffic flowing. And stopping. And flowing. And stopping.

- **Green Light.** Proceed through the intersection if it is clear of obstructions. If it is **not** clear, lean on your horn until it **is** clear.

- **Stale Green Light.** When an upcoming traffic light has been green for a long time, the defensive driver will slow down to anticipate the light turning red. You should speed **around** the defensive driver to catch the green.

- **Yellow Light.** As a traffic light turns from green to yellow, the following are expected to proceed through the intersection: Either...

    A) 6 full-sized cars

    B) 11 compact cars

    C) 37 sports cars

    D) 0 tourists

- **Red Light.** Come to a complete stop. Look in all directions for any police officers. If none are in sight, gun it.

- **Blue Light.** This means you didn't look hard enough when stopped at the **Red** light. (Or you accidentally drove into a K-Mart.)

- **Flashing Red or Yellow Lights.** You are having a brain seizure. Quickly drive to the nearest hospital.

- **Arrows.** If you encounter arrows while driving, always follow them. They will usually direct you to someone's garage sale.

MALFUNCTIONING SIGNALS

Occasionally, you will be waiting at a red light for an abnormally long period of time (i.e. more than ten seconds). If you feel that the light is malfunctioning, you may carefully proceed through it.

If there is a vehicle in front of you, you can start coaxing **them** to go through it by inching forward, tapping on your horn a bit, and giving them an acknowledging nod that says "It's okay— I'm with you." Of course, if they start to proceed through the intersection and just then, you spot a cop, by all means **Stop,** and let the other guy get the ticket.

Note: If you are approaching a light which is red and green simultaneously, be sure you're not looking at a city Christmas decoration.

OFFICER DIRECTING TRAFFIC

In some instances, a police officer will be directing traffic through an intersection. The traffic light should be ignored at these times. You may also ignore the officer if you wish. Because he's on foot, he can't catch you. And he's too busy to write down your license number. **And** he's not allowed to shoot you. (Exception: LAPD)

DRIVERS' SIGNALS

To be a safe and responsible driver, you should be familiar with the full array of drivers' hand signals....

Left Turn
To learn the hand signal for a left
turn, you can pretend that your arm is
a mobile perch for a fast bird. Keep
in mind, however, that this hand
signal makes you look very stupid.
Your best bet is to either use your
blinker, or avoid left turns.

Slow or Stop
This arm position is similar to receiving the baton
in a relay race. Or accepting money confidentially.
Or walking like one bad dude.

Right Turn

Unfortunately, this signal can often be confused with the times you put your hand out the window and cup your palm to catch the wind. But on the good side, it can be used to give "high fives" to other drivers as you pass each other on narrow bridges.

Drying Fingernail Polish

"What the Hell Was *That* Move"

You Idiot!
Universal signal.
No explanation necessary.

You Jerk!
(Los Angeles Freeways Only)

SPEED LIMIT REGULATIONS

All public roads have a particular speed limit to help ensure a safe driving environment. You should note the speed signs along the roadway, then add 30% to the posted number. This way, you will blend in safely with the traffic flow. (Few situations are more dangerous than an automobile traveling as slow as 55 mph in a 55 mph zone.)

On the other hand, when you see a vehicle approaching you from behind traveling much too fast (i.e. faster than you), you can slow him down by beginning to drift into his lane, making him think you don't see him. He'll slam on his brakes, and you'll have done your good duty of the day by thwarting a **real** speeder.

Always remember that you are required to adjust your speed to match the particular driving conditions at any time. For instance, if you are traveling on a newly-paved, unmarked, unlit highway at midnight in dense fog, you may want to reduce your speed from 85 mph to 84 mph.

The speed at which you feel comfortable driving is a matter of personal choice. If you prefer driving at slower speeds, that's okay, but stay off the expressway. In fact, stay off the roadway. In fact, it would probably be best if you stay the hell away from the rest of the population. Move to Montana and limit your driving to tractors. On Sundays.

PAVEMENT MARKINGS

The markings on the pavement can be very helpful when driving. For instance, long road trips can be made more enjoyable by studying the road kill, and trying to determine what kind of animal was flattened, **when** it was flattened, and by what type of vehicle.

The lines painted on the road can also help guide you in unfamiliar territory.

– **A Solid Yellow Line** means any or all of the following:

   A) You may not pass.

   B) You may not turn.

   C) The guy in front of you couldn't find a bath-room in time.

– **A Solid White Line** means you are in Miami driving behind a coke dealer whose trunk is leaking.

– **A Broken Yellow or White Line** means your state is in deep financial trouble, and has had to cut back half the money allocated to pavement paint.

– **Crosswalk Lines** are the parallel lines which create an imaginary "safety zone" for pedestrians to cross the street. At an intersection, it is your job as a driver to stop **in** the crosswalk area, forcing pedestrians to detour **around** your car. You're allowed to smile at them, but you can't laugh.

Crosswalk lines can also be placed across a road where there is no intersection to stop traffic. Since vehicles are usually heavier and faster than pedestrians, it is your responsibility as a driver to come to a stop when people are attempting to cross. Or at the very least, you should attempt to weave **between** the people.

USE OF LANES

Different lanes on the street are designed for different pur-poses. Observing these rules will aid in the overall flow of traffic, and will greatly reduce your chance of being shot at by fellow motorists.

– **The Passing Lane.** The left lane of a multi-lane highway is reserved for those vehicles passing other traffic. Unfortunately, this rule is ignored by a large percentage of slow drivers (also known as "Dorks"), who don't have the slightest idea they're infuriating those trying to pass.

The faster driver must resort to the dangerous practice of passing on the right, while simultaneously turning to the left to see what kind of a dork is trudging along in the passing lane. Despite thousands of drivers staring at the dork, honking at the dork, and flashing their high beam lights at the dork, the dork is in a world of his own, and will remain oblivious to his environment forever.

– **The Car-Pool Lane.** To encourage energy conservation through car-pooling, many states have created a car-pool lane, or exclusive lane, on expressways. This lane generally moves at a brisk pace.

To drive in this lane, you must have a specified number of occupants in the car—usually two. However, the particular number depends on the state. In California, you must have seven occupants, plus the driver. In Iowa, you need only one-half an occupant, **including** the driver.

The definition of an occupant also varies from state to state. In Delaware, a blow-up doll qualifies as an occupant, as long as it is fully-dressed and wearing eye make-up. In Minnesota, a dog qualifies as an occupant. (Minnesota lawmakers plan to change this rule soon, as they were recently informed by animal trainers that there weren't any actual energy savings since a dog couldn't drive by himself anyway.)

– **The Two-Way Left Turn Lane.** A relatively new concept, this is a long, single lane that runs down the center of a street, and allows vehicles from both directions to pull into it to make a left turn. It's best not to travel extended distances in this lane, as you may have an equally stupid person doing the same thing from the other direction, resulting in the fusion of metal.

– **The Emergency Lane.** This lane is typically to the right side of the road, and is more narrow than a normal lane. It is reserved exclusively for emergency situations, as well as for drivers who don't feel like waiting in traffic jams.

– The **"People Who Are Trying To *Get* Somewhere"
Lane.** While still on the drawing board, this concept
would set aside at least one lane on any multi-lane road
for people who are in their cars actually trying to get
somewhere, as opposed to those persons just out for a
leisurely drive. Any drivers found in this special lane who
are creeping along with nowhere to go and nothing to do
would be ticketed, arrested, and brought to the police
station to have their 8th Amendment rights ("No cruel or
unusual punishment") violated.

CHANGING LANES

When changing lanes, you must first turn your head to
make sure there are no vehicles beside you. Looking in your
mirrors alone is not sufficient, unless you have one of those mir-
rored balls hanging inside your car. In that case, you **can** see
everything around you, though everything will look broken.
Your regular mirrors are not sufficient because they have blind
spots. If your mirrors are old, they may also have cataracts.

It is best to change only one lane at a time, especially on the
highway. When you are seen driving "diagonally" across seven
lanes, fellow drivers may think you've suffered a heart attack at
the wheel. When they see you're fine, they'll **wish** you had suffered a heart attack.

The cautious driver also uses his or her turn signal when
changing lanes. However, since the cautious driver amounts to
about .01% of the population and "people who drive for blocks
without knowing their blinker is on" account for **65%** of the
population, it may actually be dangerous to confuse nearby
drivers by ever using your turn signal.

CHANGING CLOTHES

Just like changing lanes, you will occasionally need your
car for changing **clothes**—as a "dressing room" when you're
away from other facilities. For changing clothes, it is best to

drive to the middle of a crowded parking lot, beep your horn a few times as a fair warning, and then drop your pants.

TURNS

According to many state DMV's, there are seven steps to making a good turn. We know of one.

1) Decide you're going to turn long before the actual maneuver. (Abrupt, last-minute turns cause accidents as well as stained car seats.) By planning your turn in advance, you can slow down and keep your car from rolling over like a youthful otter in water.

Other than that, turning is pretty straightforward. So to speak.

Note: If you see a car with its turn signal on, chances are it's going straight.

Note: If you see a car **without** its turn signal on, chances are it's turning.

U-TURNS

A U-turn can help you get to a place on the opposite side of the road when a median strip prevents you from turning left. When there is no median, the U-turn is the vehicular equivalent of saying "Whoops."

You should exercise special caution when making a U-turn in an area which has a "No U-Turn" sign. Keep repeating in your mind, "But I didn't see the sign, officer."

THE THREE-POINT TURN

When you need to turn your car around (180 degrees) in a narrow area, you should use what's known as the Three-Point Turn.

66

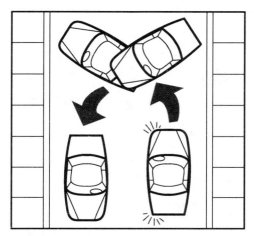

Three Point Turn

THE THIRTEEN-POINT TURN

When **elderly** drivers need to turn their car around (180 degrees) in, well, **any** area, they generally use the Thirteen-Point Turn.

Thirteen Point Turn

EXPRESSWAY DRIVING

When entering the Expressway, Highway, Freeway, or United Way, you must merge into existing traffic. That means slipping your car in front of someone whose newest goal in life is to keep you from getting in front of him. With enough practice and a lot of chutzpah, you will be able to merge into traffic with only minor dents and scratches.

Keep in mind that expressways are designed for fast travel. The following are not allowed on these roadways: Pedestrians, bicycles, animals, scooters, animals **on** scooters, Pogo sticks, and Gremlin Hatchbacks.

When leaving the expressway, wave goodbye to your fellow motorists, and head for the exit ramp. Do not begin to decelerate until you are completely out of traffic and approaching the red light thirty feet ahead at sixty miles per hour.

Some expressways have "Emergency Stopping Only" signs. While you may certainly pull over if, for example, your car is on fire, you may not pull over for a quick game of flag football.

Also, NEVER BACK UP on an expressway—unless you miss your exit. In that case, you can back up in the lane you're currently driving in, provided you toot your horn and make that "Boy-am-I-embarrassed" face.

And never try to enter an expressway ramp if you see the signs "Wrong Way" or "Stop—Do Not Enter." All right, maybe **once,** just to see the look of shock on the faces of the people heading toward you, but never again after that.

EMERGENCY STOPPING

If you must stop on the roadway, pull completely out of traffic and off the road. In order to alert other vehicles to your presence, use your flashers. (You can do this by either pushing your "Hazard" switch, or asking your passengers to stand facing traffic and expose themselves.)

PASSING

...Cute members of the opposite sex. Slowly look their way, in a laid-back yet sharp manner, and give a subtle sign of acknowledgment. (Warning: Anything involving the tongue is **not** considered subtle.)

...Gas. Remember to lower your windows, or have the air-conditioning vent on "Fresh" rather than "Re-circulate." (Unless you wish to have fun with your passengers, in which case you should totally ignore this advice.)

...Out. Being conscious is a prerequisite to driving (except in Texas). If, while driving, you feel like you're about to pass out from something such as being overtired, pull off to the side of the road immediately, walk around the car, pinch yourself, slap your face, close the trunk lid on your head a few times, hit yourself with the tire jack, put the car in reverse and quickly lie down behind it, etc. Now, feeling more refreshed and alert, you can resume driving.

NIGHT DRIVING

You must use your headlights when driving between the hours of sunset and sunrise, or when singing "Sunrise, Sunset." It is important that you don't overdrive your headlights. This occurs when you can't stop within the distance that your lights are shining ahead of your car. In fact, if you were driving at night at the speed of light, your headlights wouldn't illuminate **anything** in front of your car, so you wouldn't be able to see anything. But, of course, that's why we have speed limits.

FOLLOWING DISTANCE

When you are following another vehicle, you should stay far enough behind it so you could come to a safe stop at any time. There are several ways of figuring out a safe following distance.

70

1) Leave one vehicle length between you and the vehicle in front of you for every ten miles per hour you are traveling. (**Note:** This method is not foolproof. If you're going 60 mph and coming up on a car going 5 mph, you're history.)

2) When the vehicle ahead passes a mark, count two seconds. If you pass that mark before you're finished counting, you're following too closely. (**Note:** You can significantly reduce your following distance by counting really fast.)

3) Estimate the number of green peppers that could fit inside the car in front of you, if filled to the roof. Divide that number by the square root of your car's age, and multiply that quotient by 47. The resulting number means nothing, but you will have had to keep at a safe distance while doing all that math in your head. (Maybe that Trig class **isn't** such a bad idea.)

STOPPING DISTANCE

You must be able to stop your vehicle within the specific distance mandated by your state. For your own safety, keep in mind that various conditions can affect your stopping distance:

- Inclement weather.
- The condition of your brakes and tires.
- The time since your last cup of caffeine-rich coffee.
- Extra weight in your vehicle (i.e. Aunt Bertha).
- How many other drivers saw the armored car accidentally drop a money sack in the road.

RAILROAD CROSSINGS

When your car is approaching a railroad crossing at the same time as a train, the train has the right-of-way. You will know railroad tracks are ahead of you and a train is approaching by: bright yellow advanced warning signs; pavement markings with two R's and an X; a crossbuck that says "Railroad Crossing"; large red flashing lights; a loud clanging bell; and long striped gates which lower into the middle of the street.

Note: Don't be confused by a bright yellow sign with **three** X's. That means you're approaching an adult book store.

If you fail to notice all of these warnings, or try to drive around the gates to beat the train, you'll probably become a human pancake. A dead human pancake.

Remember that when approaching a railroad crossing where traffic prevents you from completely crossing the tracks, it is extremely dangerous and rather stupid to stop on the tracks. If a train begins heading toward you and you have nowhere to move, it will once again be pancake city.

SAFETY BELTS

Most states now require the driver and front-seat passenger of cars to wear safety belts, or seat belts. In an accident, these simple devices can save your life by keeping you from re-creating the human cannonball act at the circus.

NOT Wearing Safety Belts

Wearing Safety Belts

For the belts to be effective, it is important that you wear them properly.

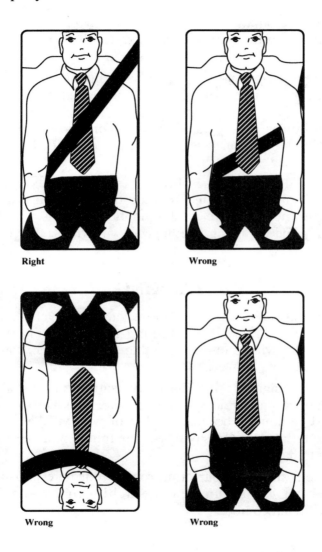

Right   Wrong

Wrong   Wrong

Of course, once the seat belt sign goes out, feel free to move about the car as you wish.

CHILD RESTRAINT DEVICES

A secured car seat is required for the adequate protection of any babies or small children riding in your car. Unfortunately, even with all of the laws and safety research, a small contingent of stupid parents still do not harness their kids when driving.

For those who have trouble understanding what happens in an accident, try to grasp this: A 20-pound infant in only a 20 mph crash becomes a 400-pound force. To make matters worse, if that baby has a dirty diaper, there's going to be a 400-pound "load" flying into your face. That would be avoided with a child restraint device.

Also, don't confuse child restraint devices with those "leashes" some parents use to keep track of their kids. These leashes are not effective in automobile accidents. On the contrary, they end up acting like huge yo-yo strings. *(See Games to Play with Kids)*

PARKING

Parking is an important part of your motor vehicle training. In the most simple terms, parking means pulling over to a secluded area with your date, shutting off the engine, and participating in heavy petting....

- Begin by engaging in light conversation, talking about the weather, recently-released movies, etc. This verbal exchange should be simple, because neither of you will have any idea what you're actually saying—your minds will be on what's going to happen next.

- For men, slipping your arm around your date is usually the next step. This can best be achieved by the famous yawn/stretch combo.

(For further steps, please consult the Unabridged Driver's Handbook, located in your state's capitol building.)

PARKING ON A HILL

To keep your car from rolling when parked on a steep hill, turn your wheels toward the curb when facing downhill, and away from the curb when uphill.

To re-create every comedy film ever made in San Francisco, do the opposite.

PARKING OVER THE HILL

(See Elderly Drivers)

PARALLEL PARKING

Your best bet is to just drive a few more blocks and find a straight or angled parking space.

PULLING OUT

(See the Unabridged Driver's Handbook)

Note: If you're stopped in traffic and someone wants to pull out in front of you from a driveway, simply pretend like you have absolutely no peripheral vision and can't see them waving their arms at you. If they beep their horn, pretend you're also deaf.

NO PARKING ZONES

All states have areas in which parking is prohibited. The following is a list of the more common "No Parking" areas.

- In front of a driveway.
- Within 15 feet of a fire hydrant.
- In a space reserved for the disabled.
- Within 8 feet of any guy named "Guido."
- On the flower garden of a police officer.

- Over an open manhole in which men are working.
- On your neighbor's cat.
- At the entrance of Bloomingdale's the morning of their "75% Off Sale" on Ladies' Shoes.

PARKING BY DISABLED PERMIT

Most parking lots have special spaces reserved for disabled drivers. These spaces are found closest to the building. You may park in these spaces ONLY if you have a special permit, or if you're in a **really** big hurry.

Disabled permits can be obtained through the DMV. Counterfeit permits (for those in a really big hurry) can be obtained through mail-order, under names such as *Ronco's New Park-Wherever Decals,* just $8.99 plus $4.50 P&H. Or in Tijuana at $5 per hundred. (**Note:** If anyone happens to be looking when you park with a fake decal, simply limp into the mall.)

TOLL BOOTHS

Roads that have tolls are an important part of the state's revenue system. It's the state's way of saying, "Either give us your spare change, or go 219 miles out of your way. Your choice."

If the toll booth has a gate which opens when you deposit money, you must be patient while the machinery processes your coins, and 35 seconds later, opens the gate for you. If you are in a rush, you should just crash through the gate like they do in the movies.

When an automated booth does **not** have a gate, there are three ways to proceed:

A) Slow down and toss your coins into the basket.

B) Slow down and make an arm motion, **pretending** to toss your coins in.

C) Come to a complete stop. Toss your coins toward the basket. Miss the basket. Open your door. Look for your coins on the ground. Ignore the cars beeping behind you. Get out of your car and down on all fours. Hold up traffic for an eternity.

Note: Tossing your coins in the basket would be considered the proper procedure. Tossing your cookies in the basket would not.

CHAPTER FIVE

YOUR VEHICLE

To maximize your driving enjoyment, it is important that you become very familiar with your motor vehicle—not in a perverted sense or anything, but just so you know your camshaft from your injector nozzles.

You may even wish to give your vehicle a nickname. In fact, it's **mandatory** in Mississippi. With the proper knowledge of your vehicle, you'll even be able to find it in crowded mall parking lots in under forty-five minutes.

MAXIMUM SIZE OF VEHICLE

Your car must conform to standards set by the federal government. If any object hangs outside of the vehicle, you must attach a red caution flag to it.

MAXIMUM SIZE OF DRIVER

You must conform to standards of normalcy and decency, especially if driving to the beach. If any body part hangs outside of the vehicle, you must attach a red caution flag to it.

MANDATORY EQUIPMENT

The law requires that your vehicle have certain basic equipment, such as an engine. (Hyundais are exempt.) Some states require additional equipment. For example:

• New York requires working seat belts in the trunk.

• Michigan requires a "Made in America" label somewhere on the vehicle.

IN GEORGIA, GUN RACKS AND
CONFEDERATE FLAGS ARE REQUIRED.
THE PIG IN THE BACK IS OPTIONAL.
SOMETIMES SHE'LL WANT TO
RIDE UP FRONT.

- Idaho requires a supply of No Doz in the glove compartment.
- Wyoming requires airbags.
- New Jersey requires dirtbags.
- Georgia requires a confederate flag and a gun rack on all trucks.
- Vermont requires a picnic basket somewhere in the car.
- Louisiana requires a bumper sticker that reads—"Ask Me About the Grandchildren My First Cousin and I Have."

OPTIONAL EQUIPMENT

In most states, you are permitted to have extra equipment in or on your vehicle. This equipment can include:

– **Mobile Phone.** As previously mentioned, this is a dangerous toy in the car, because it takes your mind off the road. Especially if you accidentally dial a "900" sex service.

– **Dangling Furry Dice.** These must not block your view...just like your black velvet painting of Elvis at home doesn't block your windows.

– **Vanity License Plate.** The driver with the vanity or customized license plate is often trying to say he has a secret and you don't know what it is. This is conveyed through a series of letters, numbers, and hieroglyphics which obviously mean **something,** but would require a military code expert to decipher. To put these idiots in their place, motion them over to the side of the road. Then say, "What the hell does your license plate mean?!" Their next license plate is guaranteed to make more sense.

– **CB Radio.** While nothing is actually wrong with having one, it does tell the world that you're probably not a member of Mensa.

– **"Baby on Board" Sign.** While nothing is actually wrong with having one, it does tell the world that you're **definitely** not a member of Mensa.

- **UV (Ultraviolet) Lights Under Vehicle.** A toy for the driver who is truly desperate for attention. If you see one, make him feel really good—hand him one of your old black light posters from the 60's, and tell him that his car is the grooviest, most far out set of wheels you've seen in at least the last ten minutes.
- **8-Track Tape Deck.** Only allowed if you're wearing either bell-bottoms or a polyester leisure suit.

HOW TO HANDLE A VEHICULAR BREAKDOWN

No matter how well you maintain your motor vehicle, there's always a chance it will break down on the road. If that happens, there are several steps you should take:

- Pull completely off the roadway.
- Raise your hood. (If on a horse, raise your hoof.)
- Scream obscenities at your car while kicking your fender.
- Blame your spouse, service station, or car manufacturer, but never yourself.
- Tie a white, **unused** handkerchief to your antenna.
- If others are in the car, sing selections from "The Sound of Music."
- Lock your doors and keep your windows closed until official help arrives, or until you suffocate.

HOW TO HANDLE A *TESTICULAR* BREAKDOWN

Get rid of that ridiculous beaded car seat.

HOW TO HANDLE A *MENTAL* BREAKDOWN

Write to Ann Landers, so she can tell you to seek counseling immediately.

EXHAUST REQUIREMENTS

In order to keep our air clean, motor vehicles must conform to specific exhaust requirements. These pollution-control devices may not be tampered with, unless you live in a state like North Dakota, where there's more than enough fresh air to disperse a little pollution.

If you see a motor vehicle that is obviously violating a clean-air law, pull up next to it, put your hands to your throat, and pretend to be choking. After enough persons do this, the offending driver will either get the message, or will think he's going crazy, and check himself into a mental hospital—either way alleviating the problem.

VEHICLE INSPECTION

Many states require that your vehicle be inspected on a regular basis. Examining personnel will make sure your basic vehicular equipment is in proper working order. For an extra few bucks, they will also change your oil, rotate your tires, and tint your windows.

Some states are tougher than others during inspections. Arizona, for example, also checks your radio to see what stations you've pre-set. If any of your buttons are not set to Country music, you fail.

PREVENTING AUTO THEFT

Locking your car doors and taking the key is no longer a deterrent for the professional auto thief. As thefts involving motor vehicles continue to rise, more automobile owners are opting for anti-theft devices. Some of these gadgets include:

   – **Car Alarm.** This used to be an effective way of keeping criminals from stealing your property. However, today's average parking lot has at least five car alarms ringing simultaneously, usually sparked by something like a sneeze. People therefore now ignore the alarms, making the devices the electronic equivalent of "crying wolf."

- **Fake, Cheap, or Removable Radio.** With stereo systems being the most frequently stolen auto accessory, many drivers have tried to outsmart the criminal. This strategy generally doesn't work, and the car still ends up being vandalized. Therefore, you have two options: 1) Have no radio (Entertain yourself like you do in the shower...by **singing,** that is); or 2) Hook up your radio **directly** to the car battery, so when the thief tries to pull the system out, he receives the shock of his life. We prefer option #2.

- **Electronic Tracking Device.** Using satellite technology, this system places a radio transmitter in your car, so the vehicle can be found as soon as it is reported stolen. While this probably ruins your chance of getting any money from your insurance company, you can still have fun with the device. Future models will have a tiny speaker, so you can not only track the criminals, but you can also **talk** to them as they're driving around town in your car. For example, you can screw with their heads by pretending to be their conscience.... "Shame on you. You should know better than this...." On the other hand, you can tell them you hope they meet lots of nice ax-murderers in prison.

- **Verbal Warning Device.** This system works by sensing any movement it judges to be too close to the vehicle. When this happens, an electronic "voice" blurts out warnings such as "You are too close to the car. Move away immediately." Unfortunately, this little contraption tends to come off as having an attitude—and humans don't like machinery with an attitude. The device tends to unhinge the most stable of individuals, many of whom were simply minding their own business, walking by your car to get to theirs. Expect your car to be "keyed" on a daily basis.

CARJACKING

At one time, carjacking was what a driver did to replace a tire when it went flat.

Today, carjacking refers to a violent crime, whereby a person with no vehicle and no life attempts to forcibly acquire a vehicle from a person who is getting into or in the process of **driving** his car. This crime requires what's known as "cojones."

According to police agencies, if you find yourself becoming a victim of this crime: If you can "floor it" to escape, you should, even if it means breaking traffic laws. (And who can resist legally breaking the law.)

If you can't escape, give the scum your car, and pray that at the next intersection, **he'll** be the victim of a carjacking, and be yanked from the car by another scum.

CHAPTER SIX

FOREIGN DRIVERS
A CHAPTER OF THEIR OWN

Let it be officially proclaimed: Foreigners may ignore all United States driving rules. They do anyway.

(This goes double for Canadians.)

CHAPTER SEVEN

SHARING THE ROAD WITH NON-VEHICULAR & SEMI-VEHICULAR BEINGS

While you may choose a motor vehicle as your main mode of transportation, you are required to share the road with others. Bummer.

PEDESTRIANS

You must always yield the right-of-way to those on foot. By the same token, you may run over those on hand, knee, or buttock.

Because pedestrians are hard to see (unless they're grossly overweight and wearing bright fluorescent clothing—a stunning combination), you must be especially careful to watch for them.

The majority of pedestrian-related mishaps occur when we are driving through intersections, making turns, and pulling out of driveways. If you're squeamish when it comes to splattering-type accidents, close your eyes during these maneuvers.

BLIND PEDESTRIANS

In **all** driving situations, you must yield to any person carrying a white cane, or using a guide dog. If you happen to spot a **guide dog** using a white cane, **extreme** caution is necessary.

Note: Ignore the typo in the Missouri Driver's Handbook, which states: "You must yield to any person carrying a white **can**."

It is never appropriate when seeing a person with a white cane to take out your own black cane and join them for a quick vaudeville set.

PEDESTRIAN RESPONSIBILITIES

Pedestrians are **also** responsible for maintaining their lives.

Before stepping into the street to cross: Look to your left. Look to your right. Put your left foot in the street. Take your left foot out. Put your left foot in, then you shake it all about.

Pedestrians should use crosswalks whenever possible. Otherwise, you're fair game, like ducks at a carnival arcade. Whenever possible, you should use electronic crosswalk signals. These help you by making you wait for 23 minutes, and then telling you it's safe to cross. That's when you're hit by the car turning right on red.

While these signals originally said "Walk" and "Don't Walk," they are being replaced by universal symbols, one being a person walking, the other being a raised hand signaling you not to walk. If these new signs are not yet up in your area and you don't read English, the translation is as follows: "Walk" means it's okay to walk. "Don't Walk" means it's not okay to walk.

Note: The "Walk" signal means just that—walk. Don't run, skip, or dance. If you're caught doing any of these things, you'll be sent to your room without dinner. Period.

Certain states are more aggressive in pedestrian law enforcement than others. This is especially true in California, where you can actually receive a jay-walking ticket on Main Street at Disneyland.

When walking along a street, you should use a sidewalk if it is available. At no time are you permitted to suddenly leave the curb and hop into the street to test the reaction of drivers. Of

course, nobody can stop you from **looking** like you're about to jump into traffic.

For those times when a sidewalk is **not** available, you should walk toward the edge of the road, **facing** traffic. If you are on the wrong side of the street and cannot easily cross, you must walk backwards.

Lastly, if you are intoxicated, you may not walk on public roadways or sidewalks. Since you also can't drive or ride other vehicles after drinking, that leaves one alternative: horseback riding on private roads. The DMV figures that after thirty seconds of galloping with your body full of booze, you'll stay away from alcohol forever.

EQUESTRIANS

(Not to be confused with Pedestrians. To distinguish the two, one leaves a pile behind him. Hopefully the horse.)

All traffic regulations which apply to motor vehicle drivers also apply to horseback riders on public streets, except the rules about parallel parking.

As a driver, you may not beep your car horn when approaching a horse, unless you're a personal friend of the horse and just want to say "Hi."

Note: It is illegal to drive so closely behind a horse that his waving tail buffs your hood.

SKATEBOARDS AND JOGGERS AND BIKES, OH MY

Drivers must be especially cautious around people who are out for exercise and recreation. These individuals are often oblivious to their surroundings, because they are physically exhausted, and usually have headsets blasting music in their ears. They can be extremely annoying. They remind you that you haven't exercised regularly since before the first lunar landing. Depending on the particular situation, it may be okay to give them a little "wake up" bump, as long as it looks like an accident.

A common mishap involving bicycle riders and skateboarders occurs when a driver accidentally opens the door of her parked vehicle, directly into the path of the quickly-approaching individual, thereby launching said individual into extended flight. You must be careful to avoid this type of accident, as it can significantly increase your auto insurance premium.

BICYCLE RIDER RESPONSIBILITIES

If you ride a bicycle on public roads, you are subject to all of the traffic rules that apply to motor vehicles, though nobody actually expects you to follow them.

While growing up, bike riders are taught a variety of additional safety regulations, such as: Keep at least one hand on the handlebars; Only one person should be on a bike unless it's built for two; and the rule that conjures up wild thoughts in the mind of every pre-pubescent lad—Don't ride more than two abreast.

Children who follow all of these rules grow up to be accountants.

Because most bicycle riders pay no attention to traffic regulations, additional rules have been created:

- Use a bike path if available. (A bike path is a 3-inch-wide strip labeled "Bike Path," that is saturated with potholes and storm drain gratings, and can be found squeezed into the right lane of a busy roadway.)

- When riding at night, you must have a light. (That refers to illumination, not beer.)

- You may not hitch a ride by holding onto the back of a motor vehicle, unless that vehicle is hitched onto the back of a bike.

- You must have a horn or bell on your bicycle, so if you see a Mack truck heading straight for you, you can go "Beep-Beep" or "Ring-Ring."

MOTORCYCLES

While motorcycles are considered motor vehicles under the law (as are many motorcycle **riders**), there are special regulations and guidelines that the rider must adhere to.

For example, when crossing railroad tracks, motorcyclists must sometimes change their approach to go over the tracks at a direct 90-degree angle. Otherwise, their front wheel could catch in the tracks, so they'd end up proceeding **along** the tracks rather than across them. Though "riding the rails" can be fun for awhile, trains tend to spoil the joviality.

To obtain more information on this subject, most states have a separate handbook written specifically for motorcycle riders. Words are kept to two syllables or less, and there are lots of big, colorful pictures.

RECREATIONAL VEHICLES/CAMPERS

You'll be in good shape driving your R.V. across America as long as you follow all of the standard driving rules, and realize that everybody detests driving behind your big, bulky, sluggish, gas-guzzling, exhaust-fuming house-on-wheels. Happy camping.

AIRPLANES

Occasionally, you will see a story on the news about an airplane making an emergency landing on the highway. If, while driving a convertible, you spot an airplane attempting to make an emergency landing right where you're driving, you should take a flashlight in each hand and direct the plane in for a smooth landing.

Common courtesy also includes welcoming the passengers to your city, telling them the local time and temperature, and helping them with any carry-on luggage they may have stored under their seat or in the overhead compartment.

CHAPTER EIGHT

SAMPLE TEST QUESTIONS FOR THE WRITTEN DRIVER'S EXAM

Below are some sample test questions to prepare you for your written exam. Answers are supplied after each question, but are not necessarily correct.

1) What is the easiest way to change the address on your driver's license?

( ) A. Call the license office and make an appointment.

( ) B. Take a small razor blade and cut & paste the right letters/numbers to reflect your new address.

( ) C. Take one of your postal return labels and stick it onto your license.

( ) D. Move back to your old address. There **is** no easy way.

(Answer: D.)

2) True or False: If you change your sex but your name remains the same, you will **not** need a new license.

*(Answer: True. However, you **will** need a new wardrobe.)*

95

3) The best way to remove splattered, dried bugs from your car's windshield is to:

( ) A. Lick the bugs to re-moisturize them.

( ) B. Pour cooking oil all over your windshield to loosen and/or saute the bugs.

( ) C. Use your fingernails to scrape the bugs off.

( ) D. All of the above.

(Answer: D. And then suck your fingernails until they're clean.)

4) You are most likely to have an accident:

( ) A. Within 25 miles of your home.

( ) B. Within 25 miles of someone else's home.

( ) C. When your odometer reading ends in 13.

( ) D. When you are heading the wrong way down a one-way street in heavy fog, and Stevie Wonder is driving towards you.

(Answer: D. Even without the fog.)

5) What should always be part of your pre-driving check-list?

( ) A. Check to make sure your seat belt is fastened and your fly is up.

( ) B. Before backing out, look in the rear-view mirror to make sure your nose hairs are not excessively pro-truding.

( ) C. After shifting into gear, raise your hand to your mouth and check your breath.

( ) D. All of the above.

(Answer: D. And repeated at every red light.)

6) What is the maximum speed you may travel in **reverse**? (Show all work.)

( ) A. 8 miles per hour.

( ) B. 28 miles per hour, if skidding.

( ) C. The reverse of the two digits of the posted speed limit.

( ) D. The Department of Highway Safety has never issued a law regulating one's speed in reverse. You may therefore travel as fast as you wish.

(Answer: D. But don't expect full credit. You didn't show your work.)

7) Who is allowed to ride in the back of a pickup truck?

( ) A. Anyone being transported to or from his/her work place.

( ) B. Anyone named Billy Bob, Jim Bob, or Joe Bob.

( ) C. Anyone with eight or more siblings.

( ) D. All of the above, including A, B, and C.

(Answer: D.)

8) What are some of the ways to know you're getting too old to continue driving?

( ) A. When everything seems eerily quiet if no car horns are beeping at you.

( ) B. When you receive more rude hand gestures each day than supplemental insurance offers.

( ) C. When the speed difference between you driving forward and in reverse is less than 15 mph.

( ) D. When you move to Miami Beach.

(Answer: E—All of the above. Yeah, we know there's no E, but nobody said this test would be fair.)

9) True or False: It is okay to drive with your **high-beam** headlights on during daylight hours if you're in the funeral procession of a professional clown.

(Answer: False.)

10) What does "DMV" stand for?

( ) A. Dangerous Mental Void.

( ) B. Dogs Mainly Vomit.

( ) C. Definitely Missed Valedictorian.

( ) D. Do Me, Verna.

(Answer: Surprisingly enough, B.)

Bonus Question:

Your car accidentally plunges into a deep lake. Inside the car are: your parents; your sister; your brother; your lover; the President of the United States; your favorite teacher; your best friend; and Ann B. Davis (Alice) from *The Brady Bunch*. You can save only one person besides yourself. Who would it be?

( ) A. Your mom.

( ) B. Your dad.

( ) C. Your sister.

( ) D. Your brother.

( ) E. Your lover.

( ) F. The President.

( ) G. Your favorite teacher.

( ) H. Your best friend.

( ) I. Ann B. Davis.

(Answer: None of the above. For gosh sake, grab your pull-out compact disc player—it's probably not covered by your insurance.)

CONCLUSION

Congratulations! You've made it to the end in one piece (or you cheated and turned to the **back** of the book before reading through it as intended. We'll give you the benefit of the doubt and assume you've been a good little reader who started from page 1).

Now that you've read all about how idiots behave on today's roadways, we'd like to say that you are officially ready to handle every driving situation our society will throw at you.

Yes, we'd **like** to say that, but we really can't. Because no matter how well-prepared **you** are behind the wheel, the moment you pull out of the driveway, you're once again going to be sharing the road with IDIOTS!

ABOUT THE AUTHOR

Bob Glickman is a mellow, rather quiet person—until he gets behind the wheel of a car, at which time he turns into a Type-A maniac from hell. Having driven in cities from Los Angeles to Miami, Bob is an expert on Idiot Drivers.

When he's not driving himself crazy on the road, Bob is a Special Events and Entertainment Producer. He's produced and directed everything from nationally-televised college football halftime shows to "The Miami Comedy Fest" on PBS. Despite the appearance of having a legitimate career, Bob is better known for his comedy writing escapades.

His material has been seen for years on *The Tonight Show* through comedians such as Jay Leno and Joan Rivers. Bob is also an award-winning screenwriter, and the author of three other humor books—*Work Sucks!*, *The Comedy Material Sourcebook*, and *The Worst Baby Name Book*.

Bob is single, but hopes to one day find and settle down with a woman who is clearly a better driver than he is.

NOTES:

TITLES BY CCC PUBLICATIONS

Blank Books ($3.99)
GUIDE TO SEX AFTER BABY
GUIDE TO SEX AFTER 30
GUIDE TO SEX AFTER 40
GUIDE TO SEX AFTER 50
GUIDE TO SEX AFTER MARRIAGE

Retail $4.95 – $4.99
"?" book
LAST DIET BOOK YOU'LL EVER NEED
CAN SEX IMPROVE YOUR GOLF?
THE COMPLETE BOOGER BOOK
FLYING FUNNIES
MARITAL BLISS & OXYMORONS
THE ADULT DOT-TO-DOT BOOK
THE DEFINITIVE FART BOOK
THE COMPLETE WIMP'S GUIDE TO SEX
THE CAT OWNER'S SHAPE UP MANUAL
THE OFFICE FROM HELL
FITNESS FANATICS
YOUNGER MEN ARE BETTER THAN RETIN-A
BUT OSSIFER, IT'S NOT MY FAULT
YOU KNOW YOU'RE AN OLD FART WHEN...
1001 WAYS TO PROCRASTINATE
HORMONES FROM HELL II
SHARING THE ROAD WITH IDIOTS
THE GREATEST ANSWERING MACHINE MESSAGES
WHAT DO WE DO NOW??
HOW TO TALK YOUR WAY OUT OF A TRAFFIC TICKET
THE BOTTOM HALF
LIFE'S MOST EMBARRASSING MOMENTS
HOW TO ENTERTAIN PEOPLE YOU HATE
YOUR GUIDE TO CORPORATE SURVIVAL
NO HANG-UPS (Volumes I, II & III – $3.95 ea.)
TOTALLY OUTRAGEOUS BUMPER-SNICKERS ($2.95)

Retail $5.95
30 – DEAL WITH IT!
40 – DEAL WITH IT!
50 – DEAL WITH IT!
60 – DEAL WITH IT!
OVER THE HILL – DEAL WITH IT!
SLICK EXCUSES FOR STUPID SCREW-UPS
SINGLE WOMEN VS. MARRIED WOMEN
TAKE A WOMAN'S WORD FOR IT
SEXY CROSSWORD PUZZLES
SO, YOU'RE GETTING MARRIED
YOU KNOW HE'S A WOMANIZING SLIMEBALL WHEN...
GETTING OLD SUCKS
WHY GOD MAKES BALD GUYS
OH BABY!
PMS CRAZED: TOUCH ME AND I'LL KILL YOU!
WHY MEN ARE CLUELESS
THE BOOK OF WHITE TRASH
THE ART OF MOONING
GOLFAHOLICS
CRINKLED 'N' WRINKLED
SMART COMEBACKS FOR STUPID QUESTIONS
YIKES! IT'S ANOTHER BIRTHDAY

SEX IS A GAME
SEX AND YOUR STARS
SIGNS YOUR SEX LIFE IS DEAD
MALE BASHING: WOMEN'S FAVORITE PASTIME
THINGS YOU CAN DO WITH A USELESS MAN
MORE THINGS YOU CAN DO WITH A USELESS MAN
RETIREMENT: THE GET EVEN YEARS
LITTLE INSTRUCTION BOOK OF THE RICH & FAMOUS
WELCOME TO YOUR MIDLIFE CRISIS
GETTING EVEN WITH THE ANSWERING MACHINE
ARE YOU A SPORTS NUT?
MEN ARE PIGS / WOMEN ARE BITCHES
THE BETTER HALF
ARE WE DYSFUNCTIONAL YET?
TECHNOLOGY BYTES!
50 WAYS TO HUSTLE YOUR FRIENDS
HORMONES FROM HELL
HUSBANDS FROM HELL
KILLER BRAS & Other Hazards Of The 50's
IT'S BETTER TO BE OVER THE HILL THAN UNDER IT
HOW TO REALLY PARTY!!!
WORK SUCKS!
THE PEOPLE WATCHER'S FIELD GUIDE
THE ABSOLUTE LAST CHANCE DIET BOOK
THE UGLY TRUTH ABOUT MEN
NEVER A DULL CARD
THE LITTLE BOOK OF ROMANTIC LIES

Retail $6.95
EVERYTHING I KNOW I LEARNED FROM TRASH TALK TV
IN A PERFECT WORLD
I WISH I DIDN'T...
THE TOILET ZONE
SIGNS/TOO MUCH TIME W/CAT
LOVE & MARRIAGE & DIVORCE
CYBERGEEK IS CHIC
THE DIFFERENCE BETWEEN MEN AND WOMEN
GO TO HEALTH!
NOT TONIGHT, DEAR, I HAVE A COMPUTER!
THINGS YOU WILL NEVER HEAR THEM SAY
THE SENIOR CITIZENS'S SURVIVAL GUIDE
IT'S A MAD MAD MAD SPORTS WORLD
THE LITTLE BOOK OF CORPORATE LIES
RED HOT MONOGAMY
LOVE DAT CAT
HOW TO SURVIVE A JEWISH MOTHER

Retail $7.95
WHY MEN DON'T HAVE A CLUE
LADIES, START YOUR ENGINES!
ULI STEIN'S "ANIMAL LIFE"
ULI STEIN'S "I'VE GOT IT BUT IT'S JAMMED"
ULI STEIN'S "THAT SHOULD NEVER HAVE HAPPENED"

NO HANG-UPS – CASSETTES Retail $5.98

Vol. I:	GENERAL MESSAGES (M or F)
Vol. II:	BUSINESS MESSAGES (M or F)
Vol. III:	'R' RATED MESSAGES (M or F)
Vol. V:	CELEBRI-TEASE

**WARNING: DO NOT START
READING HERE.
SEVERE TIRE DAMAGE.**